a little bit of

enneagram

a little bit of

enneagram

an introduction to
the nine personality types

ASHTON WHITMOYER-OBER

STERLING ETHOS
New York

STERLING ETHOS
New York

STERLING ETHOS and the distinctive Sterling Ethos logo
are registered trademarks of Sterling Publishing Co., Inc.

Text © 2024 Ashton Whitmoyer-Ober

The reader is advised that this book is not intended to be a substitute
for an assessment by, and advice from, an appropriate legal, financial,
or mental health professional or other qualified expert.

ISBN 978-1-4549-5444-6
ISBN 978-1-4549-5445-3 (e-book)

For information about custom editions, special sales, and premium purchases,
please contact specialsales@unionsquareandco.com.

Printed in India

2   4   6   8   10   9   7   5   3   1

unionsquareandco.com

Cover and interior design by Erik Jacobsen
Cover illustration by GzP_Design/Shutterstock.com

contents

INTRODUCTION vi

1 • THE HISTORY OF THE ENNEAGRAM..................... 1

2 • WHAT IS THE ENNEAGRAM? 5

3 • HOW TO FIGURE OUT YOUR ENNEAGRAM TYPE 17

4 • INTRODUCTION TO ALL NINE ENNEAGRAM TYPES...... 21

5 • ENNEAGRAM ONE 31

6 • ENNEAGRAM TWO 39

7 • ENNEAGRAM THREE............................... 47

8 • ENNEAGRAM FOUR............................... 55

9 • ENNEAGRAM FIVE 63

10 • ENNEAGRAM SIX................................. 71

11 • ENNEAGRAM SEVEN.............................. 79

12 • ENNEAGRAM EIGHT 87

13 • ENNEAGRAM NINE 95

14 • ENNEAGRAM TYPES IN RELATIONSHIPS............. 103

15 • HOW TO USE THE ENNEAGRAM IN YOUR OWN LIFE 113

ACKNOWLEDGMENTS 116

ABOUT THE AUTHOR 117

INDEX 118

INTRODUCTION

Welcome to a journey of profound revelation and self-awareness—a journey that will lead you to understand the depths of your innermost being, untangle the intricacies of your motivations, and detail each thread of the unique tapestry that weaves together the fabric of your personality. Within the pages of this book, we embark on an exploration of the Enneagram, a transformative tool that illuminates the path to self-discovery and personal growth.

The Enneagram is a personality typing system, originating from ancient wisdom and infused with modern psychology. It originated between 2,000 and 4,000 years ago, and is one of the oldest personality systems. The Enneagram offers an insightful map of nine distinct personality types, each representing a unique way of viewing and experiencing the world. As we dive into these nine specific types, you will come to recognize the one that resonates most with your innermost being. The Enneagram differs from other personality typing systems because it doesn't show you who you are—rather, it unveils why you do things the way that you do.

You're sitting here with this book in your hand because I was once also trying to discover who I am and the way that I view the world around me. It was when life presented me with challenges both great and small that I felt prompted to question who I am and why I respond to situations in certain ways. It is in these moments that you start to realize the things that make you, you—your strengths, weaknesses, fears, and desires. This realization forms the foundation upon which the Enneagram is built. It is a system that, like a compass, guides us toward understanding ourselves and those around us on a deeper level.

Discovering the Enneagram has forever altered my life. I'm not just talking about discovering my Enneagram *type*. I'm referring to the part of the Enneagram that is much deeper, guiding us toward understanding the patterns and automatic responses that may have held us back from achieving our full potential. When we understand our motivations for doing things, we can ultimately change the trajectory of problematic behaviors that we have exhibited. This has not only changed my relationship with myself but also my relationships with those around me.

I invite you to set aside preconceived notions and embrace the Enneagram with an open heart and mind. As you immerse yourself within these pages, you will embark on a transformative journey—a journey of self-compassion, empathy, and acceptance of who you are and why you do things the way that you do. Remember, self-discovery is a lifelong adventure, and the Enneagram is but a powerful compass to guide you along the way.

Let's begin!

1
the history of
the enneagram

As we set out on this Enneagram journey, it's important to speak about the beginnings of its existence: where it came from, how it changed, and how we got here today. The Enneagram's origins are covered in mystery, so much so that we only have a range of how long ago it was discovered: between 2,000 and 4,000 years ago. While there is no definitive record of its exact beginning, it is believed that the Enneagram's ancient origins can be traced to various spiritual traditions, including Sufism, Christianity, and Kabbalah. This is why the Enneagram can sometimes be referred to as a spiritual practice. Some of the earliest references to the Enneagram are from Christian mystics who dove into the idea of nine interconnected personality types sensing the way people perceived and responded to the world around them.

It wasn't until the twentieth century that the Enneagram was brought to the Western world by George Gurdjieff. Gurdjieff, a man of profound wisdom and mystery, introduced the Enneagram as a symbol of transformation and self-awareness. Through his work, Gurdjieff helped individuals break free from the constraints of their automatic behaviors and awaken to a higher level of consciousness. The Enneagram, as a symbol of interconnectedness and inner potential, became a tool for self-study and a gateway to self-discovery.

In the second half of the twentieth century, a group of scholars and truth-seekers began researching the Enneagram's true meaning. Notably, Oscar Ichazo, a Chilean mystic and philosopher, offered key insights into the nine distinct personality types and the underlying motivations that govern our actions. His work laid the foundation for the modern Enneagram system that many of us recognize today.

Building upon Ichazo's work, renowned psychologists Claudio Naranjo and Don Riso further developed and popularized the Enneagram in the Western world. Through their research and publications, they transformed the Enneagram into a powerful tool for personal growth and transformation, resonating deeply with individuals seeking self-understanding and spiritual awakening.

And over the past several years, we've seen the Enneagram increase in popularity due to our unprecedented access to information online, as well through the introduction of social media, which gives us so many different ways to share this knowledge. But even though the Enneagram has been gaining popularity, the roots of the system remain: this tool provides individuals with an ability to identify the way in which they view the world and to use that knowledge to grow in self-awareness and acceptance.

2
what is
the enneagram?

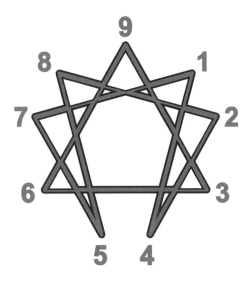

The Enneagram is an ancient typing system that contains nine different categorizations of personality—nine ways of viewing the world. The term *Enneagram* is derived from the Greek words *ennea*, which stands for *nine*, and *gramma*, which stands for a *figure* or *symbol*. The Enneagram symbol itself consists of a circle with nine points connected by lines and is often represented as a nine-pointed star within a circle. The Enneagram can be a tool for self-awareness, personal growth, and understanding human behavior.

Each of the nine Enneagram types represent a specific pattern of thoughts, emotions, motivations, fears, desires, and behaviors. The difference between the Enneagram and other personality typing systems is that your Enneagram type isn't defined by behavior characteristics. Instead, the Enneagram is about your type's motivations, which is made up of your biggest fears and biggest desires. This means that everyone could be exhibiting the same behavior, but the motivations behind that behavior could be different based on Enneagram type. The Enneagram states that people have core personality types with distinct motivations and tendencies that are present from an early age. This means that the Enneagram is more *nature* versus *nurture*. However, it also acknowledges that life experiences, upbringing, cultural influences, trauma, personal history, and such can shape how your Enneagram type manifests. For example, life experiences, such as abandonment, abuse, or any sort of childhood trauma, can contribute to how your core Enneagram type tendencies are expressed. Because of this, your core Enneagram type will stay the same throughout your life, however, your behaviors will, and should, change. Each Enneagram type has its strengths, challenges, and opportunities for growth.

THE NINE TYPES

ENNEAGRAM ONE: The Reformer

ENNEAGRAM TWO: The Helper

ENNEAGRAM THREE: The Achiever

ENNEAGRAM FOUR: The Individualist

ENNEAGRAM FIVE: The Investigator

ENNEAGRAM SIX: The Loyalist

ENNEAGRAM SEVEN: The Enthusiast

ENNEAGRAM EIGHT: The Challenger

ENNEAGRAM NINE: The Peacemaker

WINGS

Before we dive into the specifics of each Enneagram type, it's important to discuss the concept of *wings*. Wings are the numbers on either side of your main Enneagram type. Enneagram wings exist to complement your core Enneagram type. In other words, your Enneagram type can be influenced by the traits and tendencies of the types on either side of it on the Enneagram symbol. Most people might feel like one of the wings might have a stronger influence on their personality than the other; however, you have access to the traits and characteristics of both of your wings. Your wing types add layers of complexity to your core type. They can influence the way your core

type is expressed and can contribute to variations in behavior, traits, and preferences. Unlike your core Enneagram type, your wings can fluctuate back and forth, meaning that your dominant wing might be more evident in certain situations or aspects of your life.

LINES

Each Enneagram type is connected to two other types on the Enneagram symbol. One of these types is linked through a Line of Integration, also known as the Growth Line. When a person is moving along their Line of Integration, they tend to adopt some of the positive traits of the connected type. This means that when they are a healthy version of their type, they display behaviors that are characteristic of the connected type. This is a positive and constructive movement for personal development.

The other type that a person is connected to is through a Line of Disintegration. When under stress or experiencing difficulties, individuals may start to exhibit behaviors associated with the connected type along their Line of Disintegration, also known as the Stress Line. This can lead to the amplification of less healthy aspects of their personality, often causing them to act in ways that are less in line with their core type.

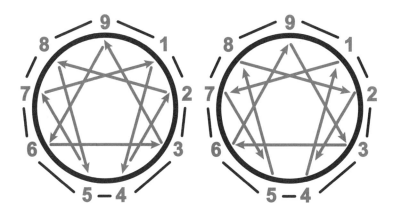

Understanding the Line of Integration and Line of Disintegration can provide valuable insights into how individuals respond to different situations and how they work toward personal growth and transformation. It's important to note that individuals can experience both integration and disintegration movements, growth, and stress over time, and these dynamics contribute to the complexity of each person's Enneagram journey.

LEVELS OF HEALTH

There are three levels of health that we use to determine the state of our personality. These levels fall on a continuum, ranging from healthy to unhealthy. Most individuals will be at an average level of health, while striving to meet the healthy standards. The levels of health provide a profound lens through which we can examine our inner landscapes and interpersonal dynamics. Understanding where we fall within this continuum allows us to recognize our tendencies, strengths, and areas in need of growth.

When someone is at the healthy level of health, they exhibit the virtues and strengths associated with their Enneagram type, fostering resilience and authentic self-expression. At the average level of health, individuals may encounter moments of insecurity, as their core fears, desires, and motivations exert their influence. At the unhealthy level of health, individuals will grapple with exaggerated traits and self-destructive behaviors. These behaviors hinder personal growth and cause distress for themselves and those around them.

CENTERS OF INTELLIGENCE

The Enneagram system also categorizes the nine types into three Centers of Intelligence. These centers represent different ways in which individuals process and respond to the world around them. Each center encompasses three Enneagram types that share common cognitive and emotional patterns.

The Gut Center contains types Eight, Nine, and One and is associated with instinctual and gut-based reactions. Individuals in this center tend to process information and make decisions based on their immediate physical and emotional responses. They often have a strong sense of their own physical presence and can be driven by concerns related to power, control, security, and autonomy. These types have a shared characteristic of anger; however, they all display it differently. Enneagram Eights view anger as a natural emotional expression, and they don't think much about it. Nines tend to bury their anger, and it in turn eats away at them and turns into passive aggressiveness. Additionally, Enneagram Ones will say that they don't get angry. Instead, they will say that they get frustrated or annoyed because they believe that it's not "right" or "correct" to be angry.

The Heart Center contains Enneagram types Two, Three, and Four and is characterized by emotional awareness and interpersonal dynamics. Individuals in this center tend to process information through their feelings and emotions, and they often seek validation and connection with others. They are driven by the need for acceptance, belonging, recognition, and a sense of identity. These types have a shared characteristic of shame. Enneagram Twos tend to feel shame when they aren't doing enough for other people, while Enneagram Threes' shame is typically related to their success or achievement. Enneagram Fours feel shame surrounding their identity and feeling like they aren't "enough" or that something is missing in them.

The Head Center contains Enneagram types Five, Six, and Seven and is centered around intellectual and analytical processing. Individuals in this center tend to process information through their thoughts and mental analysis. They often focus on issues related to safety, security, and managing uncertainty. Anxiety may be a common theme in this center, and individuals may respond by seeking knowledge, planning, and strategizing. These types have a shared characteristic of fear. Enneagram Fives tend to fear having their personal space and resources depleted. Sixes have the strongest relationship to fear because it is their main motivation. They think about fear often, and plan and prepare to avoid any of their fears coming to fruition. Sevens tend to fear being trapped in any sort of emotional pain or negativity.

Understanding your primary Center of Intelligence can provide insight into how you naturally approach challenges, make decisions, and relate to others. While your core type falls within one center, you also have access to the strengths and challenges of the other two centers. This adds depth to your self-awareness and personal growth journey with the Enneagram.

STANCES

The Enneagram system categorizes individuals into three stances: Assertive, Compliant, and Withdrawn. Each stance reflects a different way of relating to others and the world. Individuals can use the stances to uncover how they respond to others and their environment.

The Assertive Stance contains Enneagram types Three, Seven, and Eight. These types are oriented toward the external world in a protective manner, meaning that they move against people to get their needs met. Those in the Aggressive Stance have a natural tendency to assert their needs and opinions, and they feel comfortable engaging with others. They are often dynamic, driven, and always striving for their goals. However, they might also be prone to impatience and controlling tendencies, as they can struggle with letting go of their desire to be influential.

The Compliant Stance contains Enneagram types One, Two, and Six. They are focused on fitting in with their environment and seeking validation from others, meaning that they move toward people to get their needs met. Those in the Compliant Stance are often reliable, responsible, and dependable individuals who seek approval and avoid conflict. Their need for acceptance can sometimes lead to a fear of disappointing others, which may cause them to suppress their true feelings.

The Withdrawn Stance contains Enneagram types Four, Five, and Nine. These types tend to have a more introspective orientation. They tend to withdraw from immediate interactions to process their thoughts and feelings internally, meaning that they move away from people to get their needs met. These individuals tend to prefer observing situations from a distance before engaging and value their privacy and personal space. Those in the Withdrawn Stance are incredibly insightful; however, they might also struggle with overthinking and a tendency to isolate themselves when feeling overwhelmed.

3

how to figure out your enneagram type

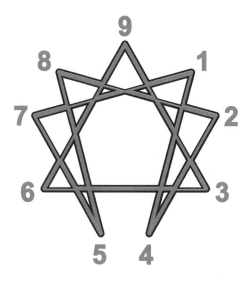

To use the Enneagram for self-discovery, it's important to first discover your Enneagram type. There are many different Enneagram tests that exist to help individuals determine their Enneagram type, but tests aren't the most accurate due to a number of reasons. For example, much of the time we answer questions on these tests based on the ways in which we want to be perceived versus how we actually are. Additionally, tests excel at scoring for behaviors, but not necessarily motivations. Taking an Enneagram test can be a great place to start, but it's important to do your own research and reflection to see what resonates with you about specific Enneagram types. Here are other ways to figure out your Enneagram type:

- Think about your core motivations. What drives you in life? What are your deepest desires? What are you most afraid of? Consider what truly matters to you and what you seek to achieve or avoid.

- Each type has a fundamental fear and desire. For instance, type One's basic fear is of being imperfect, and the desire is to be good and right. Consider which fear and desire resonates most with you on a deep level.

- Each Enneagram type displays specific patterns of behavior when stressed or in a state of growth. Reflect on how you react when you're under stress and when you're feeling more secure and in a state of growth. Do your reactions align with any particular Enneagram type?

- Enneagram types often have patterns that develop in childhood as coping mechanisms. Reflect on your childhood experiences, fears, desires, and behaviors. Were there any consistent patterns that emerged throughout your life?

Here are some questions to ask yourself that could be related to each of the Enneagram types.

For Enneagram One, ask yourself if you typically feel like there is one right way to do something.

For Enneagram Two, one thing you can ask yourself is if you naturally know how other people are feeling and what they need.

For Enneagram Three, ask yourself if you're doing things throughout the day to impress other people.

If you're trying to decide if you're an Enneagram Four, think about how you view melancholy. Does it sometimes feel like a pleasurable experience?

For Enneagram Five, is it more comfortable for you to observe life rather than fully participate in it?

For Enneagram Six, ask yourself if you constantly think about worst-case scenarios.

If you're trying to decide if you're an Enneagram Seven, ask yourself if you feel like you're constantly seeking new experiences and adventures.

For Enneagram Eight, ask yourself if you have a strong exterior that tends to intimidate other people.

If you're trying to decide if you're an Enneagram Nine, ask yourself if it's difficult for you to determine your own wants, desires, needs, and opinions and if you tend to take on the wants and needs of others.

Asking yourself these questions can help you get closer to figuring out your true Enneagram type.

Sometimes the best way to figure out your Enneagram type is simply to read in-depth descriptions of the Enneagram types and see which one resonates most with your core motivations, fears, desires, and behaviors. It's common to feel a strong connection to one or two types. As humans, we tend to want others to tell us what our Enneagram type is. However, it's important to invest in the time it takes to discover your Enneagram type and embrace the benefits that come from the deep reflection that it requires to get there.

4

introduction to all nine enneagram types

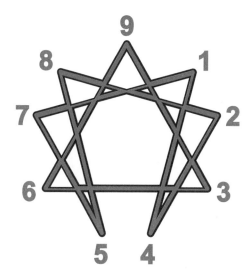

Every Enneagram type has its own title that is simply used as a place card. There are multiple titles that you may see being used to describe each Enneagram type, but I will be using titles that come from The Enneagram Institute. Here are the nine Enneagram types:

1. **THE REFORMER**

2. **THE HELPER**

3. **THE ACHIEVER**

4. **THE INDIVIDUALIST**

5. **THE INVESTIGATOR**

6. **THE LOYALIST**

7. **THE ENTHUSIAST**

8. **THE CHALLENGER**

9. **THE PEACEMAKER**

Each Enneagram type is defined by its biggest fears and biggest desires. These are called the *motivations* of each of the Enneagram types. Of course, there are stereotypical characteristics and behaviors associated with each of the Enneagram types, but it's the motivations that determine the type, *not* the behaviors. Let's dive deeper into the motivations of each of the nine Enneagram types.

ENNEAGRAM ONES are driven by a relentless pursuit of perfection and a deep-seated fear of making mistakes or being morally wrong. Their biggest motivation is rooted in the desire for integrity and the need to be right. They are often seen as principled and conscientious individuals, striving to improve themselves and the world around them.

ENNEAGRAM TWOS are characterized by their innate desire to help and care for others. Their core fear revolves around the idea of being unloved or unworthy of love. Their core motivation is the need to be needed and to gain love, approval, and appreciation through their acts of kindness and generosity.

ENNEAGRAM THREES are highly driven and success-oriented individuals. Their biggest fear is failure and worthlessness, and they are motivated by the pursuit of success, recognition, and admiration. They often excel in their careers and are driven to prove their value through their accomplishments.

ENNEAGRAM FOURS are marked by their quest for authenticity and a fear of being insignificant or lacking a unique identity. They

A LITTLE BIT OF ENNEAGRAM

also fear something being inherently wrong with them. Their biggest motivation is a deep desire to be special or unique in their own way. They tend to be introspective and often have a strong sense of individuality.

ENNEAGRAM FIVES are known for their intellectual curiosity and a fear of being overwhelmed by the world's demands and intrusions. Their biggest motivation lies in the pursuit of knowledge, understanding, and the need for competence and self-sufficiency. They are wise, objective, and innovative individuals.

ENNEAGRAM SIXES are driven by a fear of uncertainty, danger, and betrayal. They typically fear *fear* itself. Their biggest desire is to

seek security, safety, and guidance, often looking to trusted authorities for support and loyalty. They are diligent and loyal individuals who value stability.

ENNEAGRAM SEVENS are characterized by their zest for life and a fear of pain, boredom, and deprivation. Their biggest motivation is the pursuit of pleasure, excitement, and endless possibilities. However, they are ultimately seeking true contentment. They are adventurous and often seek out new experiences to avoid discomfort.

ENNEAGRAM EIGHTS are strong-willed and assertive individuals who fear vulnerability, being controlled, or manipulated. Their biggest motivation is the need for control, self-reliance, and a strong

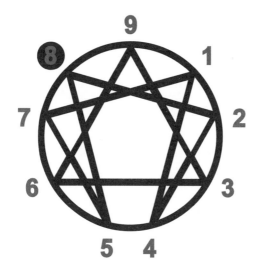

desire to protect themselves and others. They are often seen as powerful and protective figures.

ENNEAGRAM NINES are marked by their desire for peace and harmony and a fear of conflict, disconnection, and inner discomfort. Their biggest motivation is the longing for tranquility and a tendency to avoid conflicts by merging with others' desires and needs. They are often seen as easygoing and accommodating.

The purpose of the Enneagram isn't to use it to define who you are. Instead, the Enneagram should be viewed as a tool to increase personal growth, self-awareness, and a deep understanding of why you do things the way that you do and why others do things the way that they do. Ultimately, the Enneagram is meant to provide individuals with a profound framework for self-discovery, personal growth, and a deeper understanding of human nature. By identifying and exploring the nine distinct personality types, each driven by unique core fears and motivations, the Enneagram offers a path to greater self-awareness and empathy.

5

enneagram one

The Enneagram One is also referred to as The Reformer. If you are an Enneagram One, your biggest desire is to be seen as a good person; to be moral, ethical, right, and to do the right thing. Your biggest fear is being seen as a bad person, unethical, or wrong. Ones also wish that other people would also just do the right thing. Because of their desire to be right, their behaviors tend to reflect that. They set exceptionally high standards and possess an innate sense of what is right and wrong, often adhering to a strict moral code. They possess a strong sense of self-discipline and self-control, allowing them to delay gratification in pursuit of their goals. However, this discipline can sometimes lead to a tendency toward self-criticism and a critical attitude toward others. Ones are driven by a deep sense of responsibility to make the world a better place by doing their part to correct injustices and imperfections.

ENNEAGRAM ONE LEVELS OF HEALTH

When Enneagram Ones are the healthiest version of themselves, they have a strong ability to see multiple ways of doing something and are able to understand the differences between others. They are able to relax and give grace to themselves and others, and they are able to release those perfectionist tendencies. Most people operate on an average level. This means that they tend to exhibit the stereotypical behaviors of their type.

When Ones are average, they adhere to strict rules and standards and hold others to those expectations. They are also highly focused on perfection and the mistakes that they have made or the mistakes that others could potentially make.

When Enneagram Ones are at their unhealthiest state, they can be completely obsessed with imperfections. They tend to micromanage people and can be highly controlling of their environment and other people. They strongly believe that their way of doing something is the only way to do it, and they're unable to accept multiple perspectives.

ENNEAGRAM ONE WINGS

Enneagram Ones could either have a Nine wing or a Two wing. This means that their main motivation will stay with the One, but they can take on specific characteristics from the Nine and the Two. An Enneagram One with a more dominant Nine wing (written as 1w9) possesses a strong sense of principle and a desire for perfection,

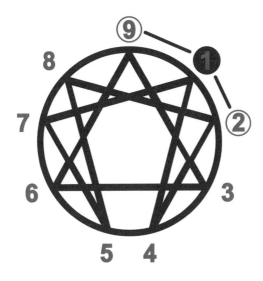

driven by a clear moral code. However, the influence of the Nine wing introduces a more laid-back and easygoing quality to their personality. They may be more patient, open to different perspectives, and inclined to seek harmony in their interactions. This combination can result in a One with a strong Nine wing being a bit less rigid in their perfectionism, more willing to compromise, and able to approach challenges with a calmer demeanor. They often strive for excellence while maintaining a preference for peaceful and harmonious relationships. An Enneagram One with a more dominant Two wing (1w2) is deeply committed to their principles and values, driven by a desire for perfection and moral correctness. However, the influence of the Two wing adds a compassionate and nurturing dimension to their personality. They are often more outwardly warm, approachable, and focused on building positive relationships. Ones with a strong Two wing are dedicated to making a difference in the world and may express their perfectionism through acts of service and support for others.

ENNEAGRAM ONE IN STRESS AND GROWTH

When stressed, Enneagram Ones will take on the unhealthy traits of an Enneagram Four. This looks like the tendency to withdraw into their emotions and become moody, depressed, or self-absorbed.

They tend to feel like no one understands them or that there is a significant piece of themselves missing. They truly feel misunderstood when stressed. Ones when stressed will also experience a lot of resentment and anger due to feeling envious of others. When in growth, Enneagram Ones will take on the healthy traits of an Enneagram Seven. This looks like stepping into positivity and having more of an optimistic outlook on life. While Ones tend to be rigid, when they are in growth they're able to be more flexible and "go with the flow." They view the glass as half full and are more spontaneous.

COMMUNICATION FOR ENNEAGRAM ONE

Enneagram Ones tend to express themselves with precision and clarity, carefully choosing their words to convey their thoughts and values. They're often seen as thoughtful and principled communicators, driven by a desire to uphold what they perceive as right and just. However, their communication style can sometimes come across as critical or perfectionistic, and they may point out areas for improvement or deviations from what they believe to be the correct path. While they strive for open and honest dialogue, they also need to be mindful of not imposing their standards on others and allowing room for different perspectives in their conversations. Overall, their communication reflects their dedication to making the world a better place by upholding their moral principles and striving for excellence.

ENNEAGRAM ONE IN CONFLICT

Enneagram Ones approach conflict with a strong sense of responsibility and a commitment to their principles. When conflict arises, they tend to experience it as a disruption to their pursuit of perfection and moral correctness. They often respond by carefully analyzing the situation, seeking to understand the root cause of the conflict, and identifying a clear course of action that aligns with their values. Ones may become more critical and perfectionistic when they are in the middle of conflict, as they want to correct what they perceive as wrong or unjust. They tend to dislike conflict, but they are willing to confront issues head-on if they believe it's necessary to uphold their principles.

Three Tips for Growth for Enneagram One

1. Acknowledge that perfection is a specific ideal that is rarely attainable in the real world. Try to learn to be more flexible and forgiving toward yourself when you make mistakes. Try to replace self-criticism with self-acceptance and self-care.

2. Practice mindfulness meditation, deep breathing exercises, or yoga as tools to help you relax and become more present in the moment. These practices can help you let go of excessive worry about the future or past and develop a greater sense of inner calm.

3. Actively seek feedback from others, and be open to different perspectives. Build a support network of friends and colleagues who can provide guidance and balance your tendency toward rigidity.

Understanding the intricate world of Enneagram Ones reveals individuals deeply committed to a quest for excellence and moral righteousness. Enneagram Ones have a strong fear of falling short of perfection, and a drive to correct what they perceive as wrong in themselves and the world. It's important for Enneagram Ones to recognize that those motivations can be demanding. Growth for Enneagram Ones calls for introspection, self-compassion, and the willingness to embrace the imperfect nature of humanity.

6
enneagram two

Enneagram Two is also referred to as The Helper. If you are an Enneagram Two, your biggest desire is to be loved, wanted, appreciated, and needed. Therefore, your biggest fear is being unloved, unwanted, and not needed. These motivations lead Twos to engage in behaviors that would allow them to feel wanted and needed, such as being caring, listening to others, practicing empathy, and helping those around them. Twos are always attuned to the needs and feelings of those around them. They possess an innate ability to nurture and support, often going to great lengths to ensure the well-being of their loved ones.

ENNEAGRAM TWO LEVELS OF HEALTH

When Enneagram Twos are the healthiest version of their type, they are truly altruistic and humble while they are doing things for others. They are helping without the expectation of something in return.

The healthiest Twos also have the ability to define and implement appropriate boundaries. This can present as self-sufficiency.

Most individuals operate at the average level for their types. When it comes to Twos, this means adhering to people-pleasing tendencies because of their desire to feel needed. As a result, they may be quick to burn out because they are always taking care of others and often neglect themselves. Some Twos may also identify with having codependent tendencies.

When Twos are unhealthy, they are self-serving and manipulative, only giving of themselves to receive something in return. They may guilt trip the people around them to manipulate them and are truly unaware of their selfish tendencies.

ENNEAGRAM TWO WINGS

As an Enneagram Two, you could either have a more dominant One wing or a Three wing. You pull characteristics from both wings, but most people will feel like they have a stronger connection to one of them. An Enneagram Two with a strong One wing (written 2w1) embodies a unique blend of qualities from both types. This individual is deeply compassionate, nurturing, and focused on helping others, driven by an innate desire to be of service because of the motivations of the Two. However, the influence of the One wing adds a strong sense of ethics, responsibility, and a commitment to doing what is right. They are principled individuals who uphold high moral standards in their caregiving and support roles. This combination

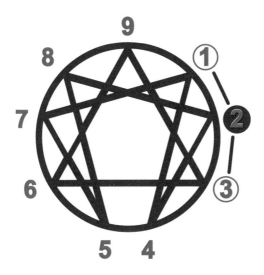

can lead to a dedicated and conscientious approach to helping others, with an emphasis on doing so with integrity and precision. Enneagram 2w1s are often seen as dependable, caring, and unwavering in their dedication to making a positive difference in the lives of those they care for.

An Enneagram Two with a more dominant Three wing (written 2w3) combines the nurturing and supportive qualities of The Helper with the ambitious and goal-oriented traits of The Achiever. This individual is highly driven to assist and care for others, seeking to be indispensable in their relationships. The Three wing adds a competitive edge and a desire for recognition and success. They are often seen as charming, adaptable, and socially adept, excelling in their ability to connect with others while simultaneously striving for accomplishment and recognition. Enneagram 2w3s are skilled at using their charisma to build networks and are often drawn to roles that allow them to make a significant impact, such as in leadership positions or careers that involve helping others while achieving personal success. They are driven by a desire to be both admired for their accomplishments and valued for their caring and supportive nature.

ENNEAGRAM TWO IN STRESS AND GROWTH

When stressed, Enneagram Twos will take on or exhibit the unhealthy

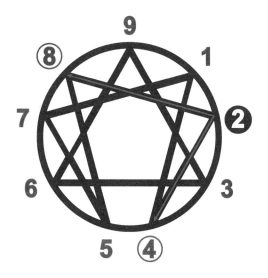

traits of an Enneagram Eight, The Challenger. This can look like lashing out with a tendency to blow up. This tends to be because of their need to regain control. Twos who are stressed will also have a tendency to blame their problems on others. When an Enneagram Two is in growth, or moving toward the healthiest version of their type, they will take on the positive qualities of an Enneagram Four. This can look like having the ability to identify and communicate their own needs and desires. They will also be more focused on creativity, passion, and truly working toward making a difference without the need for recognition.

COMMUNICATION FOR ENNEAGRAM TWO

Enneagram Twos communicate with a warm and nurturing style that reflects their natural inclination to care for others. They are excellent listeners and are quick to offer support, empathy, and assistance to those in need. Twos tend to express themselves with kindness and compassion, using their words to build connections and strengthen relationships. They often prioritize the well-being of others and may subtly steer conversations toward topics where they can offer help or support. However, Twos may also have a tendency to suppress their own needs and desires in favor of meeting the needs of others, which can sometimes lead to challenges in open and honest communication about their own feelings and needs.

ENNEAGRAM TWO IN CONFLICT

Enneagram Twos are among the specific types that tend to dislike conflict. When conflict arises, they tend to initially try to defuse the situation by offering support and understanding to all parties involved. Twos may suppress their own needs and feelings to ensure that everyone else is comfortable. However, beneath their accommodating exterior, they can feel hurt or resentful if they perceive that their efforts to help are not being appreciated or reciprocated. In resolving conflicts, Twos often strive for harmony and reconciliation, working to mend relationships and ensure that everyone is cared for. It's important for them to learn to assert their own needs and boundaries and to recognize that it's not their sole responsibility to fix every problem.

Three Tips for Growth for Enneagram Two

1. Prioritize self-care and self-compassion. Because you often focus on caring for others and may neglect your own needs, it's important to engage in self-care. Remember that self-care is not selfish but essential for your well-being. Set aside time for activities you enjoy, and learn to say no when necessary.

2. Explore and embrace your own emotions, including those you may have suppressed or overlooked in favor of caring for others. Understand that your worth is not solely tied to how much you give or do for others.

3. Set and maintain healthy boundaries with others. Because Twos have a tendency to overextend themselves to gain approval and love, it's important to communicate your needs

and limits openly and honestly with loved ones. Don't feel guilty about this!

As Helpers, Enneagram Twos are driven by an innate desire to care for and support others. We've identified their ability to be empathetic, their tendency to place the needs of others above their own, and the potential pitfalls of neglecting their own well-being. We've also discovered the beauty of their nurturing spirit and their capacity to create meaningful, lasting connections. As we move forward in this journey of self-discovery, let us remember that while Twos thrive on caring for others, it is equally vital for them to care for themselves, forging a path toward authentic and balanced relationships that honor both their generous hearts and their intrinsic worth.

7
enneagram three

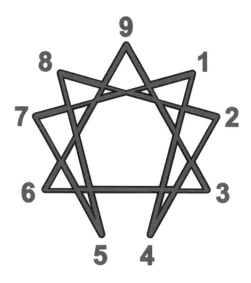

Enneagram Threes, The Achiever, are known for their tendency to value success and hard work. If you are an Enneagram Three, your biggest desire is to be seen as capable and competent and to ultimately be respected by others. Enneagram Threes fear failure the most, but then they also fear being seen as incompetent or incapable of doing something. They are often charismatic, charming, and socially adept, with a knack for making a positive impression on others. Threes are highly image-conscious and often strive to present themselves in the best possible light, which can lead to a strong focus on external achievements and success markers. While their competitive nature and dedication to their goals are commendable, it's essential to recognize that Threes can sometimes struggle with authenticity and the pressure to maintain a perfect image.

ENNEAGRAM THREE LEVELS OF HEALTH

When Enneagram Threes are living their full potential, they will exhibit healthy characteristics of their type. This can look like having the ability to be more accepting of themselves and who they are instead of others' expectations of them. They are also able to validate themselves instead of needing the external validation of others. A pivotal healthy characteristic for Threes is having the ability to slow down and just *be*, instead of the need to *do*.

When Threes are average, they constantly compare themselves and their achievements to other people. They also may struggle with a fear of failure and are highly image conscious. Average Threes are considered hardworking and motivated, but they want others to see that in them.

Unhealthy Threes have a complete loss of identity of who they are without their achievements and the different roles that they play. They have an inability to admit the mistakes that they've made or where they've gone wrong, and they can even sometimes exhibit narcissistic tendencies.

ENNEAGRAM THREE WINGS

As an Enneagram Three, you could have either a more dominant Two wing or Four wing. Remember, your motivation will stay with the Three, while you can exhibit behaviors or characteristics of the wings. An Enneagram Three with a strong Two wing (written 3w2)

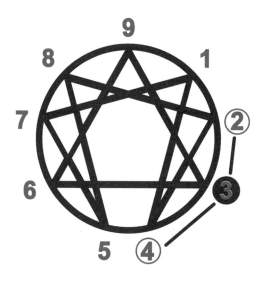

represents a dynamic blend of ambition and warmth. These individuals are highly achievement-oriented, driven to succeed and excel in their pursuits. The influence of the Two wing adds a layer of sociability, empathy, and a strong desire to be helpful to others. They are skilled at building rapport, forming connections, and using their charisma to further their goals. Threes with a dominant Two wing are often seen as confident, adaptable, and socially adept, specifically at navigating various situations with ease. They are driven by a desire to achieve recognition and success while also seeking to be admired for their caring and supportive nature. This combination can create individuals who are not only ambitious but also genuinely concerned about the well-being of those around them.

An Enneagram Three with a strong Four wing (written 3w4) embodies a unique blend of ambition and individualism. These individuals are driven by a strong desire to achieve success and recognition in their chosen endeavors. The influence of the Four wing adds depth, introspection, and a longing for authenticity to their personalities. They are often more in touch with their emotions and creative impulses, seeking to express their unique identities in their pursuits. Threes with a dominant Four wing are highly adaptable and capable of presenting themselves in a way that resonates with others while maintaining a sense of individuality. They may feel a sense of longing or a need to stand out as exceptional for their achievements. This combination can create individuals who are both ambitious and in touch with their emotions, making them capable of connecting with others on a deeper, more authentic level while still striving for success and recognition.

ENNEAGRAM THREE IN STRESS AND GROWTH

When Enneagram Threes are stressed, they will take on the unhealthy traits of an Enneagram Nine, The Peacemaker. Threes are typically intrinsically motivated, but when they are stressed, they can become procrastinators and have a hard time getting started or moving forward. They may lose interest in the things that they have typically enjoyed and can have a difficult time making decisions. When Threes are growing toward the healthiest version of their type, they

will exhibit the healthy characteristics of an Enneagram Six. This looks like the Threes becoming less competitive and more loyal to their relationships and community. They are able to slow down and are no longer defined by their achievements.

COMMUNICATION FOR ENNEAGRAM THREE

Enneagram Threes tend to be skilled communicators who convey themselves with confidence and charisma. They have a natural ability to articulate their thoughts and ideas effectively, often using persuasive and motivating language. Threes tend to be goal-oriented in their communication, focusing on achieving desired outcomes and presenting themselves in the best possible light. They are highly adaptable in various social situations, using their social intelligence to connect with others and make a positive impression. Threes may, at times, prioritize accomplishments and external success in their conversations, which can occasionally overshadow their deeper emotions or vulnerabilities. However, their ability to inspire, lead, and convey a sense of purpose makes them dynamic and influential communicators in both personal and professional settings.

ENNEAGRAM THREE IN CONFLICT

Enneagram Threes tend to dislike conflict because it gets in the way of the work that they're doing. When confronted with conflict, Threes often strive to maintain a composed and efficient demeanor, focusing on finding practical solutions and achieving a favorable outcome. They may initially downplay their own emotions, aiming to project competence and control. However, beneath this poised exterior, Threes can struggle with vulnerability and may grapple with a fear of failure or criticism. In resolving conflicts, Threes are great at assessing the situation, setting clear objectives, and working diligently to meet their goals. Because they value results and efficiency, they will often seek compromise and cooperation to reach resolutions that benefit everyone involved. It's essential for Threes to recognize the importance of addressing their own emotional needs and not solely relying on external achievements to validate their worth.

Three Tips for Growth for Enneagram Three

1. Explore who you are aside from your achievements and accomplishments. Take time for self-reflection and introspection to better understand your inner desires, values, and emotions. Remember that it's okay to be vulnerable and to share those vulnerabilities and failures with trusted individuals.

2. Prioritize rest, relaxation, and leisure activities as much as you prioritize your work and achievements. Remember that your worth is not solely defined by external success but also by your well-being and happiness. Take your well-being back into your own hands.

3. Practice setting goals that align with your authentic values and passions, rather than solely pursuing external recognition or validation. Explore what truly fulfills you on a personal level, beyond societal expectations or standards. Set intrinsic goals that focus on personal growth, creativity, or making a positive impact in meaningful ways.

As we close this chapter on Enneagram Threes, it's important to remember that they have a remarkable drive, ambition, and determination to succeed in their chosen pursuits. We've seen how they excel at presenting themselves and achieving external recognition. Yet, we've also explored the nuanced complexities beneath their polished facades—feelings of inadequacy, the quest for authenticity, and the need to balance ambition with self-care. As we wrap up this chapter, let us reflect on the extraordinary capacity of Threes to inspire and motivate, to lead and achieve, while also acknowledging the importance of embracing vulnerability and authenticity on the path to self-discovery and genuine fulfillment.

8
enneagram four

Enneagram Four is also called The Individualist. If you are an Enneagram Four, your biggest desire is to be seen as unique, special, or significant, while your biggest fear is that something is inherently wrong with you. Fours also fear that they are average with an inability to create significance or meaning in life. Because of their motivations, Fours possess a deep and complex inner world that sets them apart. Fours have an innate yearning for authenticity and a strong desire to uncover their unique identity, which can lead to a heightened sense of self-awareness and a keen ability to explore their emotions. They are often drawn to creative pursuits, using art, writing, or other forms of expression to convey their rich inner experiences. While their depth of feeling and capacity for introspection are admirable, Fours can sometimes struggle with feelings of melancholy, longing, and a sense of being different from others.

ENNEAGRAM FOUR LEVELS OF HEALTH

When Enneagram Fours are healthy, they have the ability to feel and identify a variety of emotions in themselves and others. Because of this, they are incredibly emotionally aware and available to experience others' emotions. They are compassionate, empathetic, and they have a strong ability to create significance or meaning from experiences.

Most people are at the average level for their type, and average Fours tend to internalize their feelings and emotions. They often feel like they are different from others and that there is something missing within them. Average Fours also enjoy sitting in sadness and melancholy.

Unhealthy Fours are totally unaware of their destructive tendencies. These Fours can get lost in self-loathing and become ashamed of who they are. Unhealthy Fours can also be envious of what others have and feel that they have what is ultimately missing in them. They can also become depressed and withdrawn.

ENNEAGRAM FOUR WINGS

Enneagram Fours may have either a more dominant Three wing or a Five wing. The addition of these wings will add specific components to the personality as a whole. An Enneagram Four with a strong Three wing (written 4w3) will have a blend of ambition and individuality. These individuals are inherently introspective and value authenticity, driven by a deep desire to uncover their unique identities and emotions. The influence of the Three wing adds a layer of

adaptability, a keen sense of presentation, and a drive for success. They are often skilled at presenting themselves in a way that resonates with others, seeking recognition and admiration for their creative talents and individuality. Fours with a strong Three wing are both emotionally expressive and goal-oriented, making them capable of achieving their ambitions while staying true to their artistic and introspective nature. They may experience a tension between the desire for authenticity and the need for external validation, but this combination often results in individuals who are highly creative, driven, and capable of making a lasting impact in their chosen fields and relationships.

An Enneagram Four with a more dominant Five wing (written 4w5) will represent having both emotional depth and intellectual curiosity. These individuals possess a strong drive to explore their inner worlds, seeking to understand their unique identities and emotions in intricate detail. The influence of the Five wing adds a layer of analytical thinking, independence, and a thirst for knowledge. They are often deeply introspective and introverted, drawn to solitary pursuits like writing, art, or research, which allow them to express their profound emotions and insights. Fours with a strong Five wing value their individuality and may sometimes struggle with feelings of being misunderstood. However, this combination fosters a rare blend of creativity and intellect, enabling them to produce innovative, emotionally resonant work and offer profound perspectives to the world around them.

ENNEAGRAM FOUR IN STRESS AND GROWTH

When Enneagram Fours are stressed, they will take on the unhealthy traits of Enneagram Two, The Helper. This can often look like having such a strong desire to be needed that they become needy. When stressed, they can also have codependent tendencies and become possessive of their relationships. When they are moving toward growth, Enneagram Fours will take on the positive qualities of Enneagram One. This means that a growth-focused Enneagram Four will be more structured and organized than a stressed-out Four. They are more disciplined and productive and focused on doing the right thing.

COMMUNICATION
FOR ENNEAGRAM FOUR

Enneagram Fours communicate with a depth and emotional intensity that sets them apart. They have a unique way of expressing themselves, often diving internally into their rich inner world of feelings, thoughts, and experiences. Fours are highly introspective and value authenticity, which is reflected in their communication style. They may use vivid and expressive language to convey their emotions and inner turmoil. While they have a gift for articulating their complex inner experiences, Fours can sometimes struggle with self-doubt and a tendency to focus on what's missing in their lives, which may come across as melancholic or self-absorbed. However, their ability to tap into the raw, genuine aspects of human emotions often leads to deeply meaningful and empathetic connections with others.

ENNEAGRAM FOUR IN CONFLICT

When Fours experience conflict, they tend to focus more on the emotions and feelings associated with the conflict. When faced with conflict, Fours tend to be highly attuned to their own feelings and can become introspective, exploring the nuances of their emotions in depth. They may express their emotions passionately and openly, often using expressive and creative forms of communication to convey their inner experiences. Conflict can be particularly challenging for Fours, as they may feel a heightened sense of abandonment or rejection during disagreements. In resolving conflicts, they often seek resolution through open and honest communication, striving for a deeper understanding of their own and others' emotions. Fours value genuine connections and authenticity, and they may work toward resolutions that honor their unique identities and needs. After the conflict has been resolved, Fours will value the connection that has come from the resolution.

Three Tips for Growth for Enneagram Four

1. Cultivate self-compassion and self-acceptance. Remember that it's okay to embrace your unique qualities, even if you don't always conform to societal norms. Mindfulness and self-compassion exercises can help you become more forgiving of yourself and your perceived flaws.

2. Challenge your inner critic and reframe negative thoughts into more positive and constructive ones. It's important to recognize that your worth is not solely defined by your emotions or external validation from others.

3. Creative outlets as a means of self-expression and emotional processing can be really impactful for Fours. Explore your artistic interests, whether through writing, painting, music, or other creative forms. Remember that your unique perspective and sensitivity can be powerful sources of inspiration and connection with others.

As we close this chapter on Enneagram Fours, let's remember the rich landscapes of their emotions, their need for authenticity that fuels their creativity, and their profound depth with which they experience life. We've also explored the shadows of their self-perception—the occasional sense of melancholy and the feeling of being misunderstood. As we conclude this chapter, let us celebrate the uniqueness and creativity that Fours bring to the world, their ability to express the human experience in all its complexity, and the invitation to all of us to embrace our individuality and the depth of our own emotions as a means to discover a more authentic and vibrant existence.

9
enneagram five

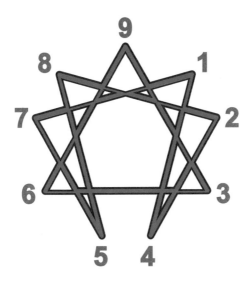

Enneagram Fives are also referred to as The Investigator. Their biggest desire is to seek knowledge and understanding in order to be seen as knowledgeable and competent. Their biggest fear is being seen as ignorant, not knowing something, or being incompetent. Because of those specific motivations, Fives are deep thinkers who love learning and exploring the world. They're often quiet and value their alone time, where they dive into their thoughts. They value their independence and autonomy, often retreating to their inner sanctuaries to recharge and process information. Fives are great problem solvers and rely on logic to make sense of things. They have a unique mix of intellect and inner introspection that sets them apart.

ENNEAGRAM FIVE LEVELS OF HEALTH

When Enneagram Fives are considered to be the healthiest version of themselves, they tend to be a master of a specific area of expertise.

They are confident in who they are and the wisdom that they possess, and they are naturally open-minded with an ability to view multiple sides and perspectives. They also have the ability to fully participate in life, rather than simply observe.

When Fives are considered average, they will be highly protective of their resources. This includes their personal space, energy, and time. They will prefer to observe life, rather than participate in it, and spend a great deal of time analyzing and processing things in their minds.

When Fives are unhealthy, they will completely withdraw from their communities. They often feel as if they are superior to other people because of their knowledge and can be more argumentative and cynical.

ENNEAGRAM FIVE WINGS

Enneagram Fives may have either a more dominant Four wing or Six wing. The purpose of the wings is for individuals to pull specific characteristics from the wings, while their motivations stay with their core type. An Enneagram Five with a strong Four wing (written 5w4) is a blend of deep thinking and emotional depth. The influence of the Four wing adds a layer of creativity, individualism, and a preference for exploring their own unique identity. They enjoy exploring ideas and their inner world, valuing their unique identity. These individuals often have a creative side, expressing themselves through art or writing. While they appreciate solitude, they may also feel like they

don't quite fit in with others. In essence, they bring together a love for knowledge and a rich emotional world, making them both introspective thinkers and creative souls.

An Enneagram Five with a strong Six wing (written 5w6) embodies a unique combination of intellectual curiosity and a strong sense of security. This individual is naturally inquisitive and seeks knowledge as a way to understand and prepare for the uncertainties of life. The influence of the Six wing adds a layer of loyalty, caution, and a desire for guidance and reassurance. They often value their close relationships and seek the wisdom and support of trusted individuals. Fives with a strong Six wing are typically meticulous in their research and planning, ensuring they are well-prepared for any situation. While they may experience anxiety or a tendency to over-think, this combination results in individuals who are both knowl-edgeable and dependable, providing a solid foundation of information and support for themselves and those around them.

ENNEAGRAM FIVE IN STRESS AND GROWTH

When Enneagram Fives are stressed, they will take on the unhealthy qualities of an Enneagram Seven. This can look like becoming scat-tered and having a hard time focusing. They will build their schedules so much that they become overwhelmed, and they can be impatient and impulsive. When they are in growth, or moving toward the

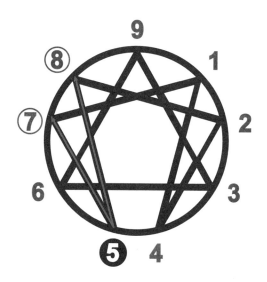

healthiest version of themselves, they will take on the positive qualities of Enneagram Eight. This can look like becoming more confident and decisive. They are also able to trust their gut and can take quick and decisive action.

COMMUNICATION FOR ENNEAGRAM FIVE

Enneagram Fives communicate with a thoughtful and reserved style. They are typically keen listeners and prefer to absorb information before sharing their own thoughts. Fives are known for their precision in language and often communicate with clarity and depth. They value intellectual discussions and may engage in conversations that allow them to share their wealth of knowledge on topics of interest. However, they can also be introverted and may need time alone to recharge after social interactions. While their communication style is thoughtful and informative, Fives may sometimes struggle with opening up emotionally, as they tend to prioritize facts and analysis over personal feelings. However, their wisdom and insights make them valuable contributors to discussions and problem-solving efforts.

ENNEAGRAM FIVE IN CONFLICT

When conflict arises, Enneagram Fives often retreat into their inner world, seeking to understand the situation intellectually and emotionally. They may take time to gather information and carefully consider their position before engaging in a confrontation. They tend to remain calm and composed, preferring logical reasoning over emotional outbursts. However, their desire for personal space and avoidance of vulnerability can sometimes lead to a delay in addressing issues. In resolving conflicts, Fives aim for a rational and objective approach, focusing on finding practical solutions and maintaining their autonomy. It's important for them to recognize the value of emotional expression and open communication in building stronger connections with others. By balancing their analytical skills with emotional awareness, Fives can navigate conflicts more effectively and foster healthier relationships.

Three Tips for Growth for Enneagram Five

1. Practice vulnerability by sharing your thoughts and feelings with trusted individuals. Remember that it's okay to let your guard down and express yourself openly.

2. Balance intellectual pursuits with practical application. Take the knowledge that you have accumulated and apply it to real-life situations to gain a richer understanding of the world.

3. Seek connections in the form of meaningful relationships and social interaction. Actively engage in social activities, even if it's in smaller, comfortable settings. Remember that connecting with others can provide emotional nourishment and broaden your perspectives.

We've explored the intellectual depths of Enneagram Fives, their insatiable curiosity, and their preference for thoughtful observation. As we close this chapter, let us appreciate the unique gifts that Fives bring—an unparalleled ability to analyze and understand the complexities of the world. While their quest for knowledge and tendency to withdraw into their inner worlds are celebrated, it's equally important to encourage Fives to balance their intellectual pursuits with emotional expression and connection. As we navigate the terrain of Enneagram Fives, let us recognize the brilliance of their minds and nurture an environment where their wisdom can flourish while gently inviting them to explore the richness of their emotional landscape for a more holistic and fulfilling life.

10
enneagram six

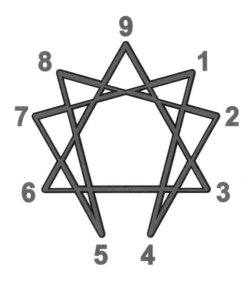

Enneagram Sixes are also called The Loyalist. Their biggest desire is to feel safe and secure in their relationships, their environments, or just in life in general. Their biggest fear is fear itself, so they actively work to rid themselves of fear. Because of these motivations, they are diligent planners, always ready for potential challenges and uncertainties that life may bring. Sixes excel at spotting potential risks and devising strategies to mitigate them. They tend to be loyal and dependable, valuing trust and forming close-knit bonds with those they hold dear. While they can sometimes wrestle with anxiety and self-doubt, these qualities also make them incredibly thorough and reliable in their pursuits. Sixes are like the safety net of our social fabric, providing stability and support when needed most.

ENNEAGRAM SIX LEVELS OF HEALTH

When Enneagram Sixes are stepping into the healthiest version of themselves, they will have the ability to trust themselves and others. Instead of being plagued by fear, they will rely on courage and strength. Healthy Sixes also enjoy collaborating with other people because of their dedication to loyalty, trust, and honesty.

Average Sixes have a strong need to be prepared at all times because of their focus on staying safe and secure. Average Sixes can become reactive and defensive during conflict, constantly questioning everything.

When they are unhealthy, they tend to find danger in everything they do. They have an inability to trust themselves and others, and they need others to make decisions for them. They can also tend to be highly anxious and panicked.

ENNEAGRAM SIX WINGS

An Enneagram Six may have either a more dominant Five wing or Seven wing. The addition of these wings will add specific intricacies to the Enneagram Six as a whole. A Six with a strong Five wing (written 6w5) represents a fascinating fusion of security-seeking and analytical thinking. This individual is naturally inclined to be loyal and committed, valuing stability and dependability in their relationships and endeavors. The influence of the Five wing adds a layer of intellectual curiosity, self-sufficiency, and a need for knowledge. They tend to approach challenges with a careful and thoughtful

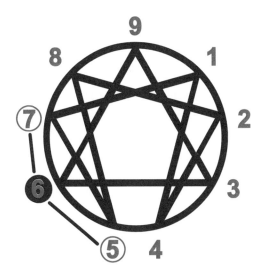

mindset, relying on their analytical skills to navigate uncertainty. They will often seek to understand the world deeply, collecting information and strategies to bolster their sense of security. While they may grapple with anxiety and a tendency to question, this combination creates individuals who are both trustworthy and well prepared.

An Enneagram Six with a strong Seven wing (written 6w7) embodies a unique blend of loyalty and a desire for adventure. This individual values security and reliability in their relationships and life choices while also seeking excitement and novelty. The influence of the Seven wing adds a layer of optimism, spontaneity, and a thirst for new experiences. They are often seen as adaptable and open to trying new things, making them sociable and approachable. Sixes with a dominant Seven wing tend to balance their cautious nature with a more adventurous spirit, and they often bring enthusiasm and a sense of fun to their endeavors.

ENNEAGRAM SIX IN STRESS AND GROWTH

When Enneagram Sixes are stressed, they will take on the unhealthy qualities of an Enneagram Three. This looks like being more arrogant and even being considered a "know-it-all." They care more about what other people think of them, and they can succumb to workaholic tendencies with an inability to rest. When Sixes are

moving toward growth, or the healthiest version of themselves, they will take on the positive qualities of Enneagram Nine. This means that they will have the ability to go with the flow because they are more secure. They will also be more empathetic and compassionate toward themselves and others.

COMMUNICATION FOR ENNEAGRAM SIX

Enneagram Sixes communicate with a cautious and methodical approach. They are typically thorough in their communication; often asking questions to gather information and ensure they understand a situation fully. Sixes value clarity and seek reassurance, so they may express their concerns or doubts when discussing various topics. They often excel in teamwork and cooperative communication, as they appreciate having a support system and allies. However, their cautious nature can sometimes lead to a tendency to overthink or anticipate problems that may not arise, which may cause them to appear indecisive. Despite this, their thoughtfulness and loyalty make them trustworthy and dependable communicators, always aiming to create a secure and stable environment in their interactions.

ENNEAGRAM SIX IN CONFLICT

When faced with conflict, Enneagram Sixes tend to be attentive to potential risks and can be somewhat anxious about the uncertainties involved. This is because conflict heightens their fear of insecurity.

Sixes may seek reassurance from trusted sources and may engage in thorough analysis of the situation. They value open communication and often express their concerns and doubts as a way of seeking clarity and safety. In resolving conflicts, Sixes typically work toward establishing a sense of stability and harmony. They may compromise and cooperate to find solutions that address everyone's needs. However, their loyalty and need for certainty can sometimes lead to indecision and overthinking. It's important for Sixes to balance their cautiousness with a willingness to trust their own instincts and judgments while also learning to manage their anxiety in conflict situations.

Three Tips for Growth for Enneagram Six

1. Work on trusting your own judgment and abilities. Recognize that you possess the inner strength and resilience to face challenges that may come your way. Self-affirmation and mindfulness techniques can help with this.

2. Challenge your catastrophic thinking patterns. Practice cognitive reframing by examining your fears and considering alternate, more positive, outcomes.

3. Take gradual steps toward facing your fears and taking risks. Start with small, manageable challenges and gradually work your way up. This will help to increase your self-assurance and develop greater resilience.

We've journeyed through Enneagram Sixes' cautious yet deeply loyal nature, their tendency to seek security, and their unwavering commitment to the people and causes they hold dear. As we wrap up this chapter, let us celebrate the steadfastness and dependability that Sixes bring to our lives, as well as their ability to foster trust and create stable foundations in a sometimes unpredictable world. While at times they may experience anxiety and doubt, let us also encourage Sixes to embrace their inner strength and self-reliance, trusting in their own abilities and finding the courage to face the uncertainties of life. In doing so, they can continue to be beacons of loyalty, support, and resilience in our communities and relationships.

11
enneagram seven

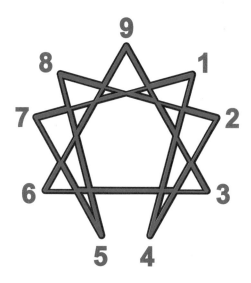

Enneagram Sevens are known as The Enthusiast. Sevens do experience the fear of missing out, but ultimately they fear being trapped in any sort of emotional pain or negativity. Their biggest desire is to have fun and to be content in everything they're doing. Because of their motivations, Sevens are eternal optimists and adventurers of life. They possess an infectious enthusiasm and an insatiable thirst for new experiences. Sevens are often the ones to infuse joy and excitement into any situation, making them great company to be around. Their minds are brimming with creative ideas, and they're always up for trying something new. However, they may struggle with staying put for too long or facing uncomfortable emotions, preferring to keep things light and positive. Sevens are the explorers of life, seeking out the next thrill or adventure on their never-ending quest for excitement and fulfillment.

ENNEAGRAM SEVEN LEVELS OF HEALTH

When Enneagram Sevens are truly the best version of themselves, they have a strong ability to be productive and focused on the present moment. They are able to accept life for how it is, including any pain and negativity that they may be experiencing. They are able to sit with their pain instead of running away from it.

When Sevens are average, they have a difficult time sitting still and being present. They are focused only on the future and the next exciting thing. They tend to reframe all negativity into positive experiences.

Unhealthy Sevens will be extremely impulsive and have an inability to pause and think things through. They may be concerned only with their own happiness and have a difficult time figuring out when to pause before moving forward. They will also do whatever they can to avoid any and all pain and negativity.

ENNEAGRAM SEVEN WINGS

An Enneagram Seven may have either a dominant Six wing or Eight wing. The influence of the wings adds different personality characteristics to the Seven as a whole. A Seven with a strong Six wing (written 7w6) incorporates a blend of enthusiasm and cautious optimism. This individual is naturally adventurous and seeks out new experiences with a sense of excitement. The influence of the Six wing adds a layer of practicality, loyalty, and a desire for security. They are

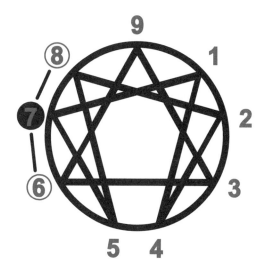

often more grounded and focused on maintaining stability in their lives and relationships. Sevens with a strong Six wing tend to balance their adventurous spirit with a need for reassurance, often seeking guidance from trusted individuals when facing uncertainties.

A Seven with a dominant Eight wing (written 7w8) is a dynamic and assertive personality. This individual combines the adventurous and enthusiastic qualities of a Seven with the self-assured and assertive traits of an Eight. They have a strong desire for independence and freedom, often pursuing their goals with determination and vigor. Sevens with a strong Eight wing are not afraid to take risks, and they approach life with a sense of boldness and self-confidence. While they are fun-loving and enjoy seeking new experiences, they are also assertive and unafraid to express their opinions. This combination makes them assertive go-getters who can inspire and lead others with their boundless energy and charisma.

ENNEAGRAM SEVEN IN STRESS AND GROWTH

When Enneagram Sevens are stressed, they will take on the unhealthy qualities of Enneagram One. This looks like being more critical and judgmental of themselves and others. They may have perfectionistic tendencies and are known to set high expectations of themselves and others. When Sevens are moving toward growth, they will take on

the healthy qualities of an Enneagram Five. Instead of the tendency to be impulsive, Sevens will instead be able to think things through before acting on them. They are more disciplined and focused and able to accept all emotions, including sadness.

COMMUNICATION FOR ENNEAGRAM SEVEN

Enneagram Sevens communicate with boundless energy and a zest for life. They are known for their upbeat and optimistic style, often infusing enthusiasm into their conversations. Sevens enjoy exploring new ideas and possibilities, making their communication vibrant and engaging. They tend to be future-oriented, focusing on opportunities and exciting ventures rather than dwelling on problems. While their enthusiasm is contagious and their creativity shines, Sevens may occasionally avoid discussing deeper emotions or uncomfortable subjects, preferring to keep things light and positive. Nonetheless, their ability to inspire and motivate with their contagious optimism makes them captivating and enjoyable communicators.

ENNEAGRAM SEVEN IN CONFLICT

When confronted with conflict, Enneagram Sevens may initially attempt to avoid or minimize it, seeking to maintain a positive and enjoyable atmosphere. Sevens are future-oriented and tend to focus on finding solutions and possibilities rather than dwelling on problems. They are skilled at reframing situations and may use humor or enthusiasm to defuse tension. However, their avoidance of negative emotions can sometimes hinder a deep exploration of the underlying issues. In resolving conflicts, Sevens often prioritize compromise and a focus on moving forward with a sense of adventure. It's important for them to recognize the value of addressing deeper emotions and challenges, allowing themselves and others to experience a full range of feelings, which can lead to more authentic and meaningful resolutions.

Three Tips for Growth for Enneagram Seven

1. Embrace moments of stillness and presence. Mindfulness meditation and grounding techniques can help you stay in the present instead of seeking future experiences.

2. Practice acknowledging and processing a full range of emotions. Allow yourself to feel and express sadness, anger, or discomfort instead of avoiding or numbing those feelings.

3. Set realistic and attainable goals instead of constantly chasing excitement and novelty. Focus on a few meaningful pursuits rather than spreading yourself too thin.

While exploring more about the Enneagram Seven, we've discovered their optimism, their love for new experiences, and their ability to infuse life with excitement. As we conclude this chapter, let us celebrate the infectious enthusiasm and creativity that Sevens bring to the world—their ability to turn ordinary moments into extraordinary adventures. While they may sometimes shy away from deeper emotions, let us also encourage Sevens to embrace the beauty of the present moment and acknowledge the full spectrum of feelings. In doing so, they can continue to inspire us with their zest for life while also finding fulfillment in the richness of authentic, heartfelt connections.

12
enneagram eight

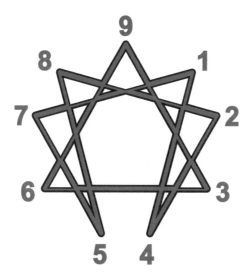

Enneagram Eight is often known as The Challenger. An Enneagram Eight's biggest desire is to protect themselves and other people, specifically vulnerable populations. Their biggest fear is being seen as weak, powerless, or controlled in some way. Therefore, their behaviors reflect a desire to be seen as strong and capable. Enneagram Eights possess a strong desire for control and autonomy, valuing their independence above all else. They are unafraid to confront challenges head-on and are often seen as protectors and advocates for those they care about. Eights have an innate ability to cut through ambiguity and speak their minds with candor and assertiveness. However, their intensity can sometimes be mistaken for aggression, and they may struggle with vulnerability and a fear of being controlled by others. In essence, Enneagram Eights bring strength, resilience, and a relentless pursuit of justice to our understanding of human personalities.

ENNEAGRAM EIGHT LEVELS OF HEALTH

When Enneagram Eights are moving toward the healthiest version of themselves, they are extremely effective and influential leaders. They have an ability to be vulnerable and show emotions while being empowering and encouraging to others. Healthy Eights are truly the voice for the voiceless.

When Eights are average, they want to be in control of their environment. They can be more confrontational and argumentative with a strong desire to protect their own emotions. They can be forceful in their opinions and ideas.

When Eights are extremely unhealthy, they can become addicted to the power that they have. They will ignore others' feelings and emotions and demand that other people follow along with what they want them to do, feel, or believe. Unhealthy Eights are known to be dictatorial, focusing on how they can control others.

ENNEAGRAM EIGHT WINGS

Enneagram Eights may have either a dominant Seven wing or Nine wing. The purpose of the wings is to add specific behavior characteristics to one's Enneagram type to explain their personality entirely. An Enneagram Eight with a strong Seven wing (written 8w7) has a captivating fusion of strength and enthusiasm. This individual exudes a natural confidence and assertiveness, making them unafraid to take charge and confront challenges head-on. The influence of

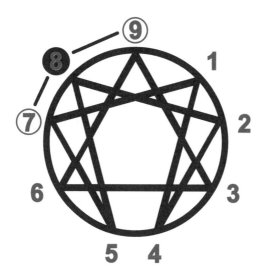

the Seven wing adds a layer of zest for life, spontaneity, and a love for new experiences. They approach life with a fearless, adventurous spirit, seeking excitement and opportunities for growth. Eights with a dominant Seven wing are known for their ability to blend their assertive nature with a sense of fun and charisma, often rallying others to join them on their quests. However, they may need to be mindful of impatience and a tendency to rush into things without careful consideration.

An Enneagram Eight with a dominant Nine wing (written 8w9) can almost create a contradictory personality type. These individuals possess the natural assertiveness and self-assuredness characteristic of Eights while also incorporating the peace-loving and conflict-avoidant qualities of Nines. They often exude a calm and composed presence, remaining unflappable even in challenging situations. They value harmony and stability, seeking to create an environment where conflicts are minimized. While they have a strong sense of self and the desire to take charge, they can also be patient and open to others' perspectives.

ENNEAGRAM EIGHT IN STRESS AND GROWTH

When Enneagram Eights are stressed, they will take on the unhealthy qualities of an Enneagram Five. Stressed-out Eights are

known to withdraw and isolate themselves from other people. They will remove themselves from their emotions completely and be more distrustful of others. When they are moving toward growth, they will take on the positive qualities of an Enneagram Two. They will be completely altruistic, putting others first at all times. They will be more empathetic and compassionate toward others, while having the ability to be more vulnerable and show their feelings.

COMMUNICATION FOR ENNEAGRAM EIGHT

Enneagram Eights communicate with directness and assertiveness. They are straightforward and value honesty in their interactions, preferring to get to the point without unnecessary fluff. Eights are natural leaders who express their opinions and intentions clearly, often taking charge of conversations or situations. They have a strong presence and can be persuasive, making them effective communicators in both professional and personal contexts. However, their directness can sometimes come across as intimidating or aggressive, and they may need to temper their assertiveness with active listening and consideration of others' perspectives.

ENNEAGRAM EIGHT IN CONFLICT

When confronted with conflict, Enneagram Eights tend to confront it head-on, expressing their opinions and concerns without hesitation. They do not shy away from conflict. Eights value honesty and may become more forceful when they perceive injustice or a threat to their boundaries. While they strive for resolution, their assertiveness can sometimes escalate conflicts. In resolving conflicts, Eights often focus on finding practical solutions and may be willing to compromise to reach an agreement. However, they may need to work on actively listening to others' perspectives and considering their feelings to ensure a balanced and fair resolution.

Three Tips for Growth for Enneagram Eight

1. Embrace vulnerability and allow yourself to express your emotions openly. Practice sharing your thoughts and feelings with a trusted individual.

2. Practice active listening and using that skill to be open to others' perspectives. This can foster more meaningful connections and strengthen your relationships as a whole.

3. Reflect on your natural assertiveness and tendency to act quickly. Take moments to pause and consider the potential consequences of your actions.

As we have discussed, Eights bring a unique and essential perspective to our understanding of human personalities, embodying the courage to face challenges head-on and advocate for justice. As we navigate the terrain of Eights, let us celebrate their formidable qualities while encouraging them to embrace vulnerability and empathetic understanding in their interactions. By doing so, they can harness their incredible strength to create more balanced, harmonious, and meaningful connections with others, paving the way for personal growth and fulfillment.

13
enneagram nine

Enneagram Nine is also called The Peacemaker. As its name suggests, a Nine's biggest desire is to maintain a peaceful environment for themselves and the people around them. Enneagram Nines tend to fear conflict the most, but they also fear being separated from the people they love. This leads to Nines valuing tranquility and disliking conflict, often going to great lengths to avoid confrontation. They possess a deep empathy and a willingness to listen to others, making them wonderful mediators and friends. However, their desire for peace can sometimes lead to a tendency to avoid their own needs and opinions, blending into the background to maintain harmony. In essence, Enneagram Nines bring a sense of serenity and balance to our understanding of human personalities, reminding us of the importance of finding inner peace amid life's complexities.

ENNEAGRAM NINE LEVELS OF HEALTH

When Enneagram Nines are experiencing the highest levels of health, they are able to fully trust themselves and truly vocalize their desires, needs, and opinions. They are able to see multiple perspectives, and they are well-versed in bringing people together.

Most people are operating at an average level of health, and when Nines are average, they tend to be accommodating because of their fear of conflict. This means they may deny their own needs because of a desire to please others, and they may even act like their own problems don't exist.

When Nines are extremely unhealthy, they will freeze in the face of conflict. They can be dependent on others and completely unaware of their identity. They might also be extremely unmotivated and procrastinate to numb themselves from the world.

ENNEAGRAM NINE WINGS

An Enneagram Nine may have either a dominant Eight wing or One wing. These are types that might seem to be the opposite of the Nine, but in reality, their tendencies allow the Nines to strengthen those qualities in themselves. An individual who is an Enneagram Nine with a dominant Eight wing (written 9w8) combines the natural desire for harmony and avoidance of conflict characteristic of Nines with the self-confidence and directness associated with Eights. Enneagram 9w8s have a remarkable ability to remain calm and diplomatic in most situations, but they can assert themselves when necessary. They

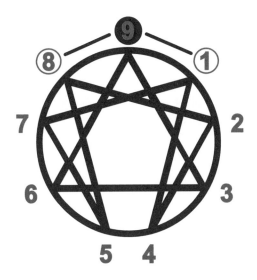

tend to be peacemakers who are unafraid to express their opinions when they sense a need for it. While they prioritize harmony and tranquility, they also have the strength to stand up for their beliefs and protect their boundaries. This combination results in individuals who are both adaptable and resilient.

An Enneagram Nine with a strong One wing (written 9w1) will have behavior characteristics of the One, while staying with the motivation of the Nine. They value tranquility and seek to maintain a balanced and just environment, often serving as mediators in disputes. They possess a natural sense of ethics and strive for integrity in their actions. While they can be accommodating, they also have a firm sense of right and wrong, making them advocates for fairness and justice. This combination results in individuals who are both adaptable and principled, striving to create a harmonious world while upholding their moral compass and sense of responsibility.

ENNEAGRAM NINE IN STRESS AND GROWTH

When stressed, Enneagram Nines will take on the unhealthy qualities of Enneagram Six. They may have a strong inability to trust themselves and other people, and they will think about worst-case scenarios. Nines who are stressed will also experience more worry and self-doubt and will find the need to be defensive. Nines who are in

growth, or moving toward the healthiest version of themselves, will take on the positive qualities of an Enneagram Three. This looks like being more motivated and focused on setting and achieving goals. They may have more of a focus on self-development and a strong ability to voice their own thoughts and opinions. Healthy Nines will confidently and passionately show up for themselves and others.

COMMUNICATION FOR ENNEAGRAM NINE

Enneagram Nines prioritize maintaining a sense of calm and unity in their interactions, often avoiding conflict and confrontation. Nines are excellent listeners and have a natural empathy, making them great at defusing tension and mediating disputes. They value harmony and often express their opinions in a nonconfrontational manner, striving to keep the peace. However, their desire to avoid conflict can sometimes lead to passive-aggressive behavior or a tendency to suppress their own needs and opinions. It's important for Nines to learn to assert themselves and express their thoughts and feelings openly while continuing to foster their remarkable talent for creating an atmosphere of tranquility and understanding in their relationships.

ENNEAGRAM NINE IN CONFLICT

When faced with conflict, Enneagram Nines may initially suppress their own needs and opinions, seeking to keep the peace and prevent tension. This is to avoid the conflict altogether. However, when forced to experience conflict, Nines tend to be patient and accommodating. They are skilled at listening to others' perspectives and finding common ground. They avoid aggressive or confrontational approaches, preferring a gentle and conciliatory style. However, their avoidance of conflict can sometimes lead to passive-aggressive behaviors or a tendency to disengage from difficult conversations. In resolving conflicts, Nines often prioritize compromise and finding solutions that accommodate everyone's needs. It's important for them to assert themselves when necessary and express their own feelings and desires openly, ensuring that their voice is heard in the pursuit of balanced and genuine resolutions.

Three Tips for Growth for Enneagram Nine

1. Voice your opinions and needs more assertively. Express yourself openly, even when it feels uncomfortable.

2. Practice setting and maintaining healthy boundaries in both personal and professional relationships. Identify your limits and communicate them clearly to others. This helps prevent feelings of being overwhelmed and ensures that their needs are respected.

3. Actively pursue personal goals and aspirations. Practice taking the initiative in areas that bring you joy and fulfillment, whether it's a hobby, career advancement, or personal development.

It's important to remember that Nines offer a valuable lesson in the art of finding unity and tranquility amid life's complexities. Their ability to create an atmosphere of calm and their empathetic nature serve as reminders of the importance of harmony and understanding in our relationships and communities. As we conclude this chapter, let us appreciate the wisdom Nines bring in fostering peace and their innate talent for mediation. Encouraging them to assert themselves and embrace their desires while preserving their gift for creating harmony can lead to more empowered and fulfilled lives. In essence, Enneagram Nines inspire us to seek balance and unity, both within ourselves and in the world around us.

14
enneagram types
in relationships

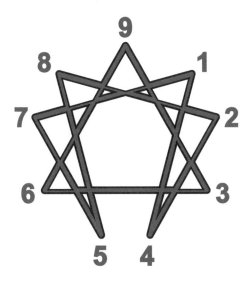

While the Enneagram is extremely helpful for self-awareness, it can be even more impactful for our relationships. This is because it can help us understand our relationships better. Once we understand what motivates us to behave in certain ways, we can be more understanding of others' behaviors. This section of the book explores how the Enneagram can improve our understanding, empathy, and connections with those who matter most to us. Whether you want to strengthen existing bonds or form new ones, the Enneagram's insights will guide you and help you learn how you interact with others based on your Enneagram type.

The Enneagram helps us see the difference between healthy and unhealthy relationships. Healthy relationships are marked by mutual understanding, open communication, and a deep appreciation for each other's unique strengths and vulnerabilities. Here, the Enneagram can help individuals identify and respect the differing needs, fears, and motivations of each type, allowing them to build bridges of empathy and trust. Unhealthy relationships, on the other hand, often result from unresolved issues and fears. The Enneagram helps us identify these problems and offers a path to healing and growth. It helps us become more self-aware and empathetic, so we can build healthy relationships and work on fixing the unhealthy ones. Let's talk about what each Enneagram type looks like in a relationship.

ENNEAGRAM ONE IN RELATIONSHIPS

Enneagram Ones bring a strong sense of integrity, responsibility, and a desire for order and structure to relationships. They have high standards for themselves and others, which can manifest as a dedication to their partner's well-being and a drive to improve the relationship. This type tends to be supportive and nurturing, often striving to create a harmonious and just partnership. They may be excellent at providing constructive feedback and encouraging personal growth in their partners and friends, though they must be mindful not to become overly critical. An Enneagram One in any sort of relationship is dependable and values loyalty, but they can sometimes struggle with perfectionism and a need for control. This may require open communication and flexibility from their partners and friends to maintain a healthy dynamic.

To nurture healthy and fulfilling connections, it's essential for Ones to balance their drive for perfection with empathy and flexibility. Begin by recognizing that not everything can be flawlessly controlled or corrected. Embrace self-compassion, as well as compassion for your people, and understand that they may not always meet your high standards.

ENNEAGRAM TWO IN RELATIONSHIPS

Enneagram Twos are exceptionally attentive to the needs of their loved ones and are quick to offer support and assistance. Twos thrive on nurturing and making their partners and friends feel cherished and valued. They are especially skilled at expressing affection and going above and beyond to ensure others' happiness. While their selflessness is a strength, they must also practice self-care and ensure their own needs are met. In relationships, Enneagram Twos can sometimes struggle with an overemphasis on their partner's and friends' well-being at the expense of their own, and they should learn to balance giving and receiving to maintain healthy reciprocal connections.

To maintain healthy and rewarding connections, it's essential for Twos to remember that it's okay to prioritize their own needs and well-being. While their nurturing nature is a beautiful asset, it's important to avoid overextending themselves or seeking validation through excessive giving. Set healthy boundaries and practice self-care to prevent burnout.

ENNEAGRAM THREE IN RELATIONSHIPS

Enneagram Threes are dedicated and ambitious in relationships. They bring a strong drive for success and accomplishment to the relationship itself, aiming to achieve shared goals and dreams. Threes are highly motivated and tend to be very focused on personal growth and improvement. They are often charismatic and confident, which can make the relationship exciting and dynamic. However, they may sometimes struggle with a tendency to prioritize work or external validation over emotional connection, and they must remember to cultivate authentic and meaningful bonds with their partners and friends. An Enneagram Three in any kind of relationship values admiration and affirmation but needs to balance this with open communication and vulnerability to ensure fulfilling and balanced partnerships.

To cultivate fulfilling and harmonious connections, it's crucial for Threes to make a conscious effort to be present and genuine in their interactions. While their drive and ambition are admirable, they need to remember that it's okay to show vulnerability and authenticity in their relationships. Threes need to avoid the tendency to prioritize external achievements over the emotional needs of their people.

ENNEAGRAM FOUR IN RELATIONSHIPS

Enneagram Fours in relationships bring a deep sense of emotional intensity and authenticity. They are passionate, creative, and highly attuned to their own and their partner's and friends' feelings. Fours are unique and often cultivate an environment that encourages self-expression and self-discovery. They cherish moments of depth and connection, and their relationships are marked by a strong desire for intimacy. However, they may sometimes struggle with intense emotions and a longing for idealized love, which can create challenges if they are not met. An Enneagram Four in any sort of relationship thrives on self-expression and emotional connection and needs to communicate openly with their partners and friends to ensure that their unique needs are understood and respected in the relationship.

To foster healthy and enriching connections, it's essential for Fours to balance their need for authenticity with an awareness of the feelings of others. They need to avoid falling into the trap of self-absorption or emotional intensity that can be overwhelming. Fours need to encourage open and honest communication, sharing their inner world with their people, while also being attentive to their emotional needs.

ENNEAGRAM FIVE IN RELATIONSHIPS

In relationships, Enneagram Fives appear thoughtful and intellectually engaged. They bring a deep curiosity and desire for understanding to the relationship. Fives value their independence and often cherish quiet, introspective moments, which can provide a sense of intellectual and emotional depth to the connection. They are typically good listeners and offer valuable insights. However, they may sometimes struggle with expressing their own emotions and may need to consciously work on sharing their feelings and being more present in the relationship. Enneagram Fives in any sort of relationship bring a wealth of knowledge and a strong sense of loyalty. They are happiest when they can engage in stimulating conversations and personal growth alongside their partners and friends.

To cultivate healthy and rewarding connections, it's crucial for Fives to balance their need for personal space and solitude with active engagement in their relationships. Fives need to avoid retreating into emotional detachment or intellectualizing every aspect of their relationships. Instead, Fives need to make a conscious effort to share their thoughts and feelings with their people and encourage open communication.

ENNEAGRAM SIX IN RELATIONSHIPS

Enneagram Sixes are dependable and supportive in their relationships. They bring a strong sense of commitment and loyalty to their relationships, making their loved ones feel secure and valued. Sixes are often cautious and responsible, helping to create stable and harmonious partnerships. They are excellent at troubleshooting and offering practical solutions to challenges. However, they may sometimes struggle with anxiety and doubt, which can lead to seeking reassurance from their partners and friends. Enneagram Sixes in any sort of relationship value trust and open communication and need their people to provide a sense of safety and consistency in the face of their occasional worries and uncertainties.

To nurture healthy and fulfilling connections, it's important for Sixes to recognize and manage their tendency to worry and seek reassurance. Sixes need to trust their intuition and judgment, and understand that not every situation requires exhaustive analysis. Communication is key. They need to ensure that they openly discuss their concerns and fears with their people, creating an environment of mutual support and understanding.

ENNEAGRAM SEVEN IN RELATIONSHIPS

Enneagram Sevens in relationships bring excitement and a zest for life. They are the ones who infuse their relationships with spontaneity and fun, constantly seeking new experiences and adventures. Sevens are optimistic, open-minded, and always up for trying new things, making their relationships lively and dynamic. However, they may sometimes struggle with a fear of missing out and a tendency to avoid difficult emotions. Sevens in any kind of relationship thrive on excitement and variety and need people who can appreciate their enthusiasm while also helping them navigate more serious or challenging aspects of life when necessary.

To nurture healthy and fulfilling connections, it's crucial for Sevens to balance their love for spontaneity with commitment and presence in their relationships. Sevens need to avoid the tendency to constantly seek the next thrill or escape uncomfortable emotions. They need to make an effort to embrace vulnerability and explore deeper emotional connections with their people.

ENNEAGRAM EIGHT IN RELATIONSHIPS

Enneagram Eights in relationships are strong and assertive. They bring a sense of confidence and protectiveness to their relationships, ensuring their loved one feels safe and supported. Eights are natural leaders and problem solvers, often taking charge and making things happen. They value honesty and direct communication, which can lead to an open and transparent dynamic in their relationships. However, they may sometimes struggle with a fear of vulnerability and a tendency to become controlling. An Enneagram Eight in any kind of relationship values strength and loyalty and appreciates people who can match their assertiveness while creating a safe space for emotional intimacy and sharing.

To cultivate healthy and fulfilling connections, it's important for Eights to balance their assertiveness and self-reliance with vulnerability and empathy. Eights need to avoid dominating or overpowering their people, and instead, strive to create an environment of trust and respect. Eights should practice encouraging open and honest communication, allowing both their needs and those of the people around them to be heard and acknowledged.

ENNEAGRAM NINE IN RELATIONSHIPS

Enneagram Nines in relationships are calm and harmonious. They bring a strong desire for unity and a serene presence to their relationships, creating atmospheres of tranquility and understanding. Nines are excellent at facilitating compromise and keeping the peace, making the relationship feel safe and comfortable. They value empathy and emotional connection, and their nonconfrontational nature can lead to an atmosphere of mutual respect and cooperation. However, they may sometimes struggle with avoiding conflict and asserting their own needs. Enneagram Nines in any sort of relationship value harmony and connection and thrive when their people appreciate their calming influence while also encouraging them to express their feelings and desires more assertively.

To cultivate healthy and fulfilling connections, it's important for Nines to balance their inclination to avoid conflict with assertiveness and self-expression. Nines need to avoid retreating into passive-aggressiveness or suppressing their own needs. Nines need to practice encouraging open communication and actively express their thoughts and feelings to their people.

15

how to use the enneagram in your own life

The Enneagram is a special tool that helps us understand ourselves better. It shows us why we do the things we do and how we can grow as people. But the Enneagram isn't just about labels or categorization; it's about using this knowledge as a tool for self-awareness, personal development, and fostering more meaningful connections with others. Now that we've learned about everything that the Enneagram entails, it's time to figure out how to put it into practice.

One way to use the Enneagram in your own life is to develop a greater self-awareness and to identify limiting beliefs that often operate beneath the surface of our consciousness. By identifying our Enneagram type and delving into its core fears and motivations, we gain insight into the patterns and behaviors that have shaped our lives. This heightened awareness allows us to recognize the deeply ingrained beliefs and thought processes that may be holding us back. With this knowledge, we can begin the transformative journey of challenging and reframing these limiting beliefs. Through reflection and introspection, we can gradually replace doubt and self-imposed constraints with empowerment and a renewed sense of possibility, fostering personal growth and a deeper understanding of ourselves.

Another way to use the Enneagram is to strengthen your relationships with yourself and others. The Enneagram serves as a powerful instrument for enhancing relationships, both with ourselves and with others. By gaining a deeper understanding of our own Enneagram type, we can uncover our unique strengths and challenges, fostering greater self-acceptance and self-compassion. This, in turn, allows us to navigate our inner world more effectively, making conscious choices that align with our true selves. When applied to our interactions with others, the Enneagram offers a lens through which we can appreciate their motivations, fears, and communication styles. This newfound empathy promotes more authentic and harmonious connections, as we learn to relate to people on a deeper level, appreciating their individuality. Ultimately, the Enneagram empowers us to not only embrace our own complexities but also to foster more meaningful and fulfilling relationships with the diverse tapestry of humanity.

A final way to use the Enneagram in your own life is by utilizing it to become a better version of yourself. By identifying our Enneagram type, we gain insight into our core fears, motivations, and habitual patterns of behavior. Armed with this self-awareness, we can actively work on personal growth and development. The Enneagram provides guidance on areas for improvement, allowing us to challenge limiting beliefs, embrace our strengths, and transcend self-imposed constraints. Through the integration of positive qualities from other types and the cultivation of mindfulness, we can progressively transform into more balanced, authentic, and empowered individuals. The Enneagram's wisdom empowers us to navigate life's challenges with greater wisdom, compassion, and resilience, ultimately fostering our evolution into the best versions of ourselves.

Remember that the wisdom of the Enneagram is a lifelong companion on your journey of self-discovery and personal growth. The Enneagram helps you understand yourself and others better. It's not just a tool; it's a guide to living a more authentic and harmonious life. May this journey inspire you to embrace your true self, cultivate empathy for others, and live a life rich in purpose, wisdom, and love.

ACKNOWLEDGMENTS

I am forever grateful for my husband, Derek, for his unconditional love and belief in me. I wrote this book with two kids two and under and I could not have done that without his encouragement and support. I am incredibly lucky to be able to walk through life with you.

Thank you to all of my family members who have listened to me talk endlessly about the Enneagram and who were my first students. Your encouragement has fueled my determination. Thank you to all of my dear friends who cheer me on in everything I do. Your presence in my life is a gift beyond measure.

Thank you to everyone in the Enneagram Ashton community. Your curiosity and engagement make this the most rewarding job. This community feels like family and I am grateful beyond words.

Thank you to the numerous Enneagram experts and researchers who have gone before me and whose work has informed and enriched the content of this book. Your contributions to the field have been instrumental and impactful.

Finally, thank you to Kate Zimmermann, my incredible editor, who believed in me and allowed me to continue to share the Enneagram in this capacity. Thank you for bringing my vision to life.

ABOUT THE AUTHOR

Ashton Whitmoyer-Ober is an author, public speaker, community psychologist, and certified Enneagram educator. She received her bachelor's degree from East Carolina University and her master's in community psychology and social change from Pennsylvania State University. With a desire to see relationships strengthened, she created Enneagram Ashton in early 2019. She is the author of *Enneagram for Relationships, The Two of Us: A Three Year Couples Journal,* and *The Enneagram Made Simple.* Ashton spends her days holding virtual Enneagram workshops and traveling around the country speaking to companies, organizations, and teams on how they can strengthen communication, increase understanding, and decrease conflict using the Enneagram. Visit her website www.enneagramashton .com for digital resources and courses and find her on Instagram @enneagramashton.

INDEX

A

Achiever. *See* Enneagram
  Three (The Achiever)
Assertive Stance explained,
  13–14

C

Centers of Intelligence
  about: explained, 11–12;
    Gut Center, 11;
    Head Center, 12;
    Heart Center, 11–12;
    understanding your
    primary Center, 12
Challenger. *See* Enneagram
  Eight (The Challenger)
Communication
  Enneagram One, 35
  Enneagram Two, 43
  Enneagram Three, 51–52
  Enneagram Four, 59–60
  Enneagram Five, 67
  Enneagram Six, 75
  Enneagram Seven, 83
  Enneagram Eight, 91
  Enneagram Nine, 99
Compliant Stance
  explained, 14
Conflict
  Enneagram One, 36
  Enneagram Two, 43–44
  Enneagram Three, 52
  Enneagram Four, 60
  Enneagram Five, 67–68
  Enneagram Six, 75–76
  Enneagram Seven, 83–84
  Enneagram Eight, 91–92
  Enneagram Nine, 99–100

E

Enneagram
  about: impacting author's
    life, vi–vii

definition and explanation,
  5–6
history of, vi, 1–3
motivations and, 6
purpose of, 28–29
spiritual traditions and,
  1–2
using in your own life,
  113–115
Enneagram One
  (The Reformer), 30–37
  about: figuring your type,
    17–19; Gut Center and,
    11; overview of, 22, 31
  communication for, 35
  in conflict, 36
  Levels of Health, 32–33
  in relationships, 104–105
  in stress and growth, 34–35
  tips for growth, 37
  Wings, 33–34
Enneagram Two
  (The Helper), 38–45
  about: figuring your type,
    17–19; Heart Center
    and, 11–12; overview
    of, 23, 39
  communication for, 43
  in conflict, 43–44
  Levels of Health, 39–40
  in relationships, 105
  in stress and growth,
    42–43
  tips for growth, 44–45
  Wings, 41–42
Enneagram Three
  (The Achiever), 46–53
  about: figuring your type,
    17–19; Heart Center
    and, 11–12; overview
    of, 23, 47
  communication for, 51–52
  in conflict, 52
  Levels of Health, 48
  in relationships, 106

in stress and growth, 50–51
tips for growth, 53
Wings, 49–51
Enneagram Four
  (The Individualist),
    54–61
  about: figuring your type,
    17–19; Heart Center
    and, 11–12; overview of,
    23–25, 55
  communication for, 59–60
  in conflict, 60
  Levels of Health, 56
  in relationships, 106–107
  in stress and growth,
    58–59
  tips for growth, 60–61
  Wings, 56–58
Enneagram Five
  (The Investigator),
    62–69
  about: figuring your type,
    17–19; Head Center
    and, 12; overview of,
    25, 62
  communication for, 67
  in conflict, 67–68
  Levels of Health, 63–64
  in relationships, 107–108
  in stress and growth,
    66–67
  tips for growth, 68–69
  Wings, 64–66
Enneagram Six
  (The Loyalist), 70–77
  about: figuring your type,
    17–19; Head Center
    and, 12; overview of,
    25–26, 71
  communication for, 75
  in conflict, 75–76
  Levels of Health, 72
  in relationships, 108–109
  in stress and growth,
    74–75

tips for growth, 76–77
Wings, 72–74
Enneagram Seven
    (The Enthusiast), 78–85
    about: figuring your type,
        17–19; Head Center and,
        12; overview of, 26, 79
    communication for, 83
    in conflict, 83–84
    Levels of Health, 80
    in relationships, 109
    in stress and growth, 82–83
    tips for growth, 84–85
    Wings, 80–82
Enneagram Eight
    (The Challenger), 86–93
    about: figuring your type,
        17–19; Gut Center
        and, 11; overview of,
        26–28, 87
    communication for, 91
    in conflict, 91–92
    Levels of Health, 88
    in relationships, 110
    in stress and growth, 90–91
    tips for growth, 92–93
    Wings, 88–90
Enneagram Nine (The
    Peacemaker), 94–101
    about: figuring your type,
        17–19; Gut Center and,
        11; overview of, 28, 95
    communication for, 99
    in conflict, 99–100
    Levels of Health, 96
    in relationships, 110–111
    in stress and growth, 98–99
    tips for growth, 100–101
    Wings, 96–98
Enthusiast. See Enneagram
    Seven (The Enthusiast)

F

Figuring your Enneagram
    type, 17–19

G

Growth Line. See Line of
    Integration
Growth, tips for
    Enneagram One, 37
    Enneagram Two, 44–45
    Enneagram Three, 53
    Enneagram Four, 60–61
    Enneagram Five, 68–69
    Enneagram Six, 76–77
    Enneagram Seven, 84–85
    Enneagram Eight, 92–93
    Enneagram Nine, 100–101
Gurdjieff, George, 1–2
Gut Center, 11

H

Head Center, 12
Health. See Levels of Health
Heart Center, 11–12
Helper. See Enneagram Two
    (The Helper)
History of enneagram, vi, 1–3

I

Ichazo, Oscar, 2
Individualist. See Enneagram
    Four (The Individualist)
Intelligence. See Centers of
    Intelligence
Investigator. See Enneagram
    Five (The Investigator)

L

Levels of Health
    about: explained, 10
    Enneagram One, 32–33
    Enneagram Two, 39–40
    Enneagram Three, 48
    Enneagram Four, 56
    Enneagram Five, 63–64
    Enneagram Six, 72
    Enneagram Seven, 80
    Enneagram Eight, 88
    Enneagram Nine, 96

Line of Disintegration, 9–10
Line of Integration, 8, 10
Lines
    explained, 8–10
    Line of Disintegration, 9–10
    Line of Integration, 8–9, 10
Loyalist. See Enneagram Six
    (The Loyalist)

N

Naranjo, Claudio, 2

P

Peacemaker. See Enneagram
    Nine (The Peacemaker)
Purpose of Enneagram,
    28–29

R

Reformer. See Enneagram
    One (The Reformer)
Relationships, Enneagram
    types in, 102–115
    about: overview and
        summary, 103–104,
        111
    Enneagram One, 104–105
    Enneagram Two, 105
    Enneagram Three, 106
    Enneagram Four, 106–107
    Enneagram Five, 107–108
    Enneagram Six, 108–109
    Enneagram Seven, 109
    Enneagram Eight, 110
    Enneagram Nine,
        110–111
Riso, Don Richard, 2

S

Stances explained
    about: overview of
        Stances, 13
    Assertive Stance, 13–14
    Compliant Stance, 14
    Withdrawn Stance, 14

Stress and growth
    Enneagram One, 34–35
    Enneagram Two, 42–43
    Enneagram Three, 50–51
    Enneagram Four, 58–59
    Enneagram Five, 66–67
    Enneagram Six, 74–75
    Enneagram Seven, 82–83
    Enneagram Eight,
        90–91
    Enneagram Nine,
        98–99
Stress Line. *See* Line of
    Disintegration

T

Types of Enneagram. *See also
    specific Types* (example:
    Enneagram One
    (The Reformer))
    about: overview of, 5–6,
        21–29
    figuring your type,
        17–19
    titles as place cards, 21

U

Using Enneagram in your
    life, 113–115

W

Wings
    about: explained, 7–8
    Enneagram One, 33–34
    Enneagram Two, 41–42
    Enneagram Three, 49–51
    Enneagram Four, 56–58
    Enneagram Five, 64–66
    Enneagram Six, 72–74
    Enneagram Seven, 80–82
    Enneagram Eight, 88–90
    Enneagram Nine, 96–98
Withdrawn Stance explained,
    14